The Resurrection
Is for Me

Written by **Jessica B. Ellingson** • Illustrated by **Aubrey Blackham**

CFI • An imprint of Cedar Fort, Inc. • Springville, Utah

When Jesus was upon the earth,
He preached and served with love.
He came to do His Father's will
So we could live above.

The Christ was born in Bethlehem
A long, long time ago.
He taught the people about God
And what they need to know.

Jerusalem to Galilee,
He taught them to repent.
He brought to them the word of God
Until His days were spent.

He used five loaves and just two fish
To feed all those who came.
He healed the sick and raised the dead
And lifted up the lame.

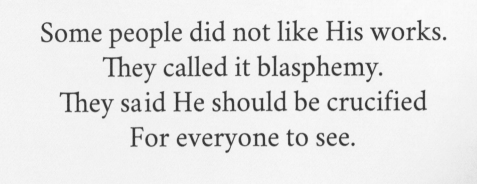

Some people did not like His works.
They called it blasphemy.
They said He should be crucified
For everyone to see.

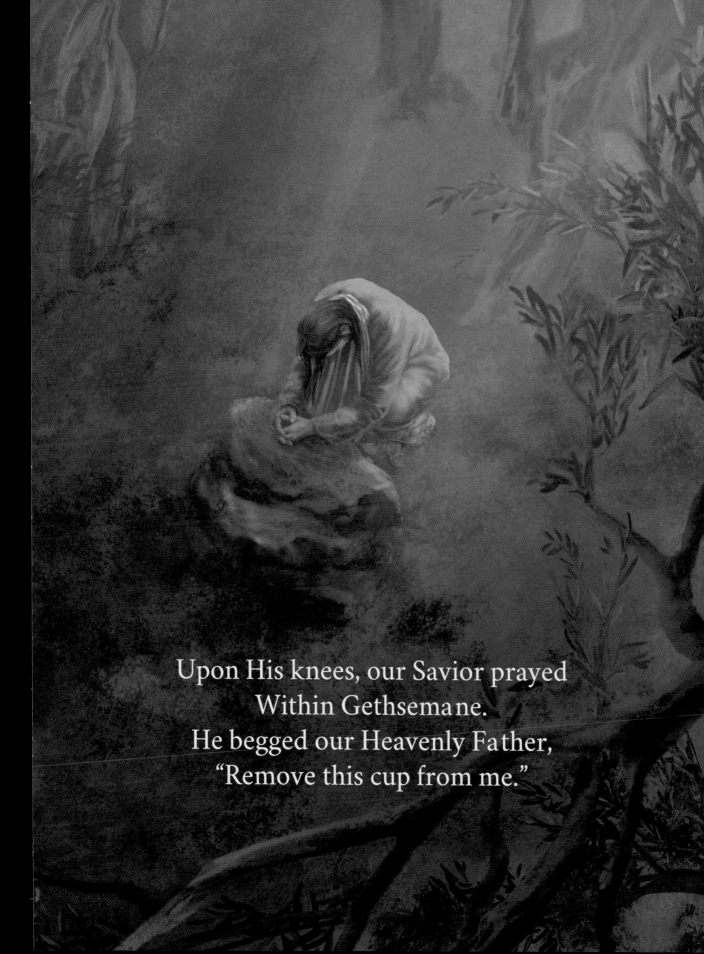

Upon His knees, our Savior prayed
Within Gethsemane.
He begged our Heavenly Father,
"Remove this cup from me."

He bore the suffering and pain
Of sins for everyone.
Our Savior then was crucified.
His Father's will was done.

But dying does not bring the end
For Him or you or me.
His Resurrection cleared the way
To live eternally.

So with the sun
on that third morn,
He rose up from the grave.

Fulfilling prophecies
of old, He then
our souls did save.

Disciples came to
tend to Him
But only found
His clothes.

For from that tomb
where Christ was laid,
Our Savior had arose.

The mighty stone was rolled away.
An angel stood nearby.
For wicked men will never win,
No matter how they try.

Christ came to
Mary at the tomb
And showed
Himself in white.

And though she
could not touch
Him then,
She did behold
His light.

Appearing to His disciples,
He showed His wounded hands:
The marks of what He did for them
To break death's bitter bands.

So through our Savior's Atonement,
We all can live again.
It fulfilled God's work and glory:
"Eternal life of man."

And like the flowers
in the spring,
Each life He will renew.

The Resurrection
is for me.
This I know is true.

To the Gray family.
We will live again.
—Jessica

To my darling children, I hope to
pass my love for the Savior to you,
as my parents did for me.
—Aubrey

ISBN 13: 978-1-4621-2322-3

Published by CFI, an imprint of Cedar Fort, Inc.
2373 W. 700 S., Springville, UT 84663
Distributed by Cedar Fort, Inc., www.cedarfort.com

   Library of Congress Control Number: 2018962233

Cover design and typesetting by Shawnda T. Craig
Cover design © 2019 Cedar Fort, Inc.
Edited by Kaitlin Barwick

Printed in the United States of America

10 9 8 7 6 5 4 3 2 1

Printed on acid-free paper